LOVE Songs

and Fragments

OF SAPPHO

Translated into English

PUBLIC DOMAIN POETS

Editor: Dick Whyte —: No. XV :— Valentine's Day 2023

SAPPHO (c. 630-570 B.C.) was born into a wealthy family from the island of Lesbos, and is said to have had 3 brothers. She probably took up poetry early in life, and would go on to become one of the most highly regarded lyric poets of ancient Greece. Sappho was exiled to Sicily around 600 BC, but continued to write until her death, circa 570. While she was known to be a prolific writer, most of her work was later destroyed by the Church, in large part because her love poetry was addressed to women:— some 10,000 lines reduced to fragments. It was translations of these incomplete verses, and specifically their (unintentional) fragmentation, which would go on to influence early 'free verse' and Imagist poets, including Edward Storer, H.D., Amy Lowell, Marie Tudor Garland (et al.). Storer, a founding member of one of the earliest English-language 'free verse' circles, went on to publish his own translations of Sappho's fragments in 1915, seemingly drawing on English-language versions of Japanese tanka and haikai as models. Other well-known translations at the time included Henry Wharton (1885), James Easby-Smith (1891), J.R. Tutin (1903), etc.

'Love Songs': Selections from James S. Easby-Smith, *The Songs of Sappho* (Georgetown University, 1891). 'Poems & Fragments': Selections from Edward Storer, *Poems & Fragments of Sappho* (The Egoist 'Poets' Translation Series', c. 1915). 'Odes & Fragments': Selections from Henry Thornton Wharton, *Sappho: Memoir, Text, Selected Renderings, & A Literal Translation* (David Stott, 1885); J.R. Tutin, *Sappho: Odes & Fragments* (self-published, 1903); Edwin Marion Cox, *The Poems of Sappho* (Williams & Norgate, 1924); C.R. Haines, *The Poems and Fragments* (E.P. Dutton, 1926). See also: Mary Mills Patrick, *Sappho and the Island of Lesbos* (Houghton Mifflin, 1912); H. de Vere Stacpoole, *Sappho: A New Rendering* (Hutchinson, c. 1918), etc.

Front & Back Cover: 'Ode from a Third Century Papyrus' (in Haines, 1926) & 'Sappho (from the bust in the Pitti Palace, Florence)' (in Cox, 1924). Inside: Illustrations, photos, & ornaments mostly from Wharton's *Sappho* (1885), etc.

This collection ©2023. All individual poems, illustrations, and ornaments belong to the 'public domain', unless otherwise noted, and may be freely copied and/or distributed. Some elements of the originals may have been marginally edited, for clarity and consistency.

PUBLIC DOMAIN PRESS
Aotearoa / New Zealand
ISBN: 978-1-7385862-3-3 (print) • 978-1-7385862-4-0 (pdf)
978-1-7385862-5-7 (kindle)

SAPPHO
LOVE SONGS & OTHER FRAGMENTS

LOVE SONGS

Fragments translated by James S. Easby-Smith,
first published 1891.

POEMS & FRAGMENTS

Fragments translated by Edward Storer,
first published 1919.

ODES & FRAGMENTS

A selection of translations and versifications,
published 1885-1926.

FOREWORD
EDWARD STORER

SAPPHO was born in the island of Lesbos about 612 B.C. Her name in her own language is "Psappha." She was a contemporary of Alkaios and Stesichoros. At some period of her life she was exiled from Lesbos. An inscription in the Parian Chronicle says: "When Aristokles reigned over the Athenians Sappho fled from Mitylene and sailed to Sicily."

But it is through her own poems that we see most clearly into the beauty and tragedy of her life. She is there revealed to us as a woman of ardent nature, noble, delicate-minded, and fond of pleasure. That her poems were chiefly love-poems, and love-poems written to women, is clear even from the mutilated fragments which remain. Any other explanation destroys at once their art and their reality. Yet sedulous hypocrites are to be found to-day who will wilfully mistranslate and misconstrue in order to envelope the manners of antiquity in a retrospective and most absurd respectability.

The grammarians of the old world say there were nine books of Sappho's poems. In addition to the fragments given here there are extant about another hundred very short fragments, sometimes of one or two words only, and the "Song of the Nereids." The bibliography of the subject is vast. In English Dr. Wharton's *Sappho* is the best modern work. There are also excellent modern versions and exegeses in French, German, and Italian.

AUTONOMOUS ELECTRUM COINS OF LESBOS
(440-350 B.C.)

LOVE Songs

Translated by
James S. Easby-Smith

FOUR GEMS SUPPOSED TO REPRESENT SAPPHO

Why, O Sappho,
   dost thou sing always of
blessed Aphrodite?

The firstling of the white goat will I
sacrifice to thee upon the altar.

They honored me by giving me their gifts.

For they to whom I have been kind
are most cruel to me.

But what this one wishes, I . . .

I will sing this that my girl-friends
may be delighted.

Towards you, fair maidens, I change not.

But their hearts were chilled and their wings were lowered.

And deep within myself do I feel this.

Let the wandering winds bear it
away, together with all care.

With many colours mingled.

But thou art forgetful of me.

Or thou lovest some man more than me.

When anger swells thy breast beware of thy sharp tongue.

They will remember us I think in the years to be.

Stand face to face beloved, and show
forth the beauty in thine eyes.

Golden vetches grew upon the shores.

Who is beautiful is good, and who is good will soon be also beautiful.

And a honey-colour settled over the lovely countenance.

And a broidered sandal of beautiful
Lydian work was bound about her feet.

Evening thou bringest all things that bright
   morning dispersed;
   thou bringest the sheep,
   thou bringest the goat,
   thou bringest the child to her mother.

They of the night, dark-eyed sleep.

Of a proud palace.

I know not which path to pursue;
my mind is at variance.

But I am fluttering, just as a child after her mother.

I do not expect to touch the sky with mine arms.

The angel of spring, the mellow-throated
nightingale.

When the long night overtook them.

Come then, sacred shell, let thy music sound for me.

Upon a soft cushion I repose.

And then softly did I spring into a thick garment.

And verily I laid the cushion down.

Come hither, thou dainty Graces and beautiful-haired Muses!

A sweet-voiced maiden.

And delicate garlands woven about a fair throat.

I do not think that another maiden as wise
shall ever behold the sunlight.

Since thou art dear to us choose a younger
companion ; for I, somewhat older,
am loath to live with thee.

Many, yea countless cups thou drainest.

I have not a spiteful temper, but preserve a quiet heart.

What country maiden steals into thy heart
who does not know how to arrange
her dress about her ankles?

But then did they weave garlands.

Come hither now O Muses, leaving the
   golden . . .

I love delicacy, and for me love shines
   with the brightness and beauty of
   the sun.

Sleep thou upon the breast of thy gentle girl-friend.

And carefully she wound about herself
delicate woolen . . .

Excelling, as the Lesbian bard excels other men.

Wealth without virtue is not a safe companion.

Ever maiden shall I be.

As a father we will give.

Do I still think upon maidenhood?

Nay, do not pride thyself upon a ring.

The bride rejoices; let the bridegroom also rejoice.

Hail bride, all hail noble bridegroom.

To what may I well compare thee, dear bride-groom?
To a tender shoot I may best compare thee.

For there was no other maiden like unto her, O bridegroom.

He seems to himself . . .

Faint not thou strong of heart.

Far whiter than an egg,

For me, nor honey nor bee.

A beautiful maiden plucking flowers.

Sweeter by far than harp, more golden than gold.

Stir not the shingle.

Ye are nothing to me.

Until ye wish.

I desire and seek . . .

A dripping napkin.

Thou burnest us.

Sweetheart.

BRONZE COINS OF MITYLENE
(350-250 B.C.)

POEMS & FRAGMENTS

Translated by
EDWARD STORER

The moon has set and the Pleiades
Have gone.
It is midnight; the hours pass; and I
Sleep alone.

I loved you once, Atthis, long ago.

He seems like a god to me the man who is near you,
Listening to your sweet voice and exquisite laughter
That makes my heart so wildly beat in my breast.

If I but see you for a moment, then all my words
Leave me, my tongue is broken and a sudden fire
Creeps through my blood. No longer can I see.
My ears are full of noise. In all my body I
Shudder and sweat. I am pale as the sun-scorched
Grass. In my fury I seem like a dead woman,
But I would dare...

I know that never again will
Look upon the sunlight
So wise a maid as you.

Who is this country girl with
Clumsy ankles and rough dresses that
Draws you towards her?

Love shakes my soul.
So do the oak-trees on the mountain
Shake in the wind.

He who is beautiful is good and soon
He who is good will be beautiful.

If you would stay with us, then choose a younger love.
A youth like yours is not for the old.

O my youth, my youth, who has you now?
I shall never know you again.

Sleep in the bosom of
Your tender friend.

I am full of longing and desire.

Unless it be you love
Another than me.

Death is evil because
If it were good, the gods
Also would die.

As the shepherd's naked feet trample the hyacinths
Upon the mountain-side until they stain the earth.

Through apple boughs the sighing winds go softly and
From the tremulous leaves sleep seems to drip.

As the apple ripening on the bough, the furthermost
Bough of all the tree, is never noticed by the gatherers,
Or, being out of reach, is never plucked at all.

Come, O goddess, come with
Delicate rare fingers, mix the
Radiant nectar in the cups of
Gold.

The stars of night gathered round the moon
    will veil their bright
Faces when she grows full and lights
    everything with silver.

Divine shell,
Your song.

Spring's messenger,
the sweet-voiced nightingale.

Fairest of all the stars.

Gold pulse flowering on the banks.

I lay my limbs upon a delicate couch.

I am well dowered by the violet-weaving Muses.

IMPERIAL BRONZE COINS OF MITYLENE
(140-190 A.D.)

Odes and Fragments

Translated into English Verse

To me the Muses truly gave
   An envied and a happy lot :
E'en when I lie within the grave,
   I cannot, shall not, be forgot.

As when in heaven the stars about the moon
Look beautiful.
                              TENNYSON.

Stars that shine around the refulgent full moon
Pale, and hide their glory of lesser lustre
When she pours her silvery plenilunar
    Light on the orbed earth.
J. A. SYMONDS, 1883.

Planets, that around the beauteous moon
Attendant wait, cast into shade
    Their ineffectual lustre, soon
As she in full-orbed majesty arrayed,
    Her silver radiance pours
    Upon this world of ours.
J. H. MERIVALE.

Through orchard-plots with fragrance crowned
　The clear cold fountain murmuring flows;
And forest leaves with rustling sound
　Invite to soft repose.
　　　　　　　　J. H. MERIVALE.

All around through branches of apple-orchards
Cool streams call, while down from the leaves a-tremble
　Slumber distilleth.
　　　　　　　　J. A. SYMONDS, 1883.

  Come, Venus, come
Hither with thy golden cup,
 Where nectar-floated flowerets swim.
Fill, fill the goblet up;
 These laughing lips shall kiss the brim,
  Come, Venus, come!
     ANON. (*Edin. Rev.* 1832).

Then, as the broad moon rose on high,
The maidens stood the altar nigh ;
  And some in graceful measure
    The well-loved spot danced round,
With lightsome footsteps treading
  The soft and grassy ground.
M. J. WALHOUSE.

The silver moon is set;
 The Pleiades are gone;
Half the long night is spent, and yet
 I lie alone.
                    J. H. M<small>ERIVALE</small>.

The moon hath left the sky;
 Lost is the Pleiads' light;
 It is midnight
And time slips by;
But on my couch alone I lie.
                    J. A. S<small>YMONDS</small>, 1883.

Sweet mother, I the web
   Can weave no more;
Keen yearning for my love
   Subdues me sore,
And tender Aphrodite
   Thrills my heart's core.
            M. J. WALHOUSE.

Evening, all things thou bringest
   Which dawn spread apart from each other;
The lamb and the kid thou bringest,
   Thou bringest the boy to his mother.
            J. A. SYMONDS, 1883.

From heaven he came,
And round him the red chlamys burned like flame.
                    J. A. SYMONDS.

When angry fires burn in thy breast,
Be quiet, calm thyself, and rest.
                    Anon. (1903).

I HAVE a child, a lovely one,
In beauty like the golden sun,
Or like sweet flowers of earliest bloom ;
And Claïs is her name, for whom
I Lydia's treasures, were they mine,
Would glad resign.
     J. H. MERIVALE.

DELICACY sweet and tender,
Unto it my heart I render.
Love, too, like the glorious sun,
Ere a cloudless day hath run,
Is beautiful, and sweet as bright,
By daylight fair, and shelt'ring night.
     ANON. (1903).

STAND before me face to face,
That thine eyes and their sweet grace
May be revealed. . . .
                      ANON. (1903).

O LOVE! thou giant strong, thou deadly thing,
Bitter, yet sweet, hast brought me suffering,
Shaking my limbs and arms.
    Why so dost cling?
                      ANON. (1903).

By Love I'm shaken, as tall trees
Are by a sudden mountain breeze.
                    ANON. (1903).

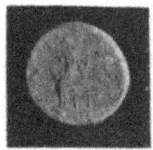

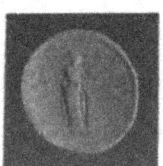

IMPERIAL BRONZE COINS OF MITYLENE AND ERESUS

This Space for Your Thoughts

Please handle with care.